Sir William Erle

The Law Relating to Trade Unions

Sir William Erle

The Law Relating to Trade Unions

ISBN/EAN: 9783744727525

Printed in Europe, USA, Canada, Australia, Japan

Cover: Foto ©Suzi / pixelio.de

More available books at **www.hansebooks.com**

THE LAW

RELATING TO TRADE UNIONS.

THE LAW

RELATING TO

TRADE UNIO

BY

SIR WILLIAM ERLE,

FORMERLY CHIEF JUSTICE IN THE COMMON PLEAS.

London:

MACMILLAN AND CO.

1869.

LONDON:
R. CLAY, SONS, AND TAYLOR, PRINTERS,
BREAD STREET HILL.

CONTENTS.

CHAPTER II.

STATUTE LAW RELATING TO TRADE UNIONS.

APPENDIX A.

APPENDIX B.

INTRODUCTION.

FOR the performance of their duty under Her* Majesty's Commission the Trade Unions Commissioners had to ascertain the state of the existing law, both Common and Statute, connected with Trade Unions, in order that amendments might be proposed with knowledge of their probable effect.

INTRODUCTION.

For this purpose I prepared the following Memorandum, with the intention of its being laid before my colleagues, and forming part of the proceedings of the Commission. It has, however, so grown under my hand as to embrace some topics beyond the immediate scope of our Commission; and I now offer it on my own responsibility.

Many of the principles were obtained by my own induction, and are expressed in words

THE LAW

RELATING TO TRADE UNIONS.

CHAPTER I.

COMMON LAW RELATING TO TRADE UNIONS.

Chap. I. Common Law.

§ 1. *Formation and Force of Unions.*

I. *Formation and Force of Unions.*—As the term "Trade Union" denotes many forms of association for various purposes—such as mutual assurance against either the accidents of life or the accidents of trade, or such as the regulation of the terms of hiring or of the supply of labour—it may be well to premise that the term itself affords no indication in respect of lawfulness. Union by itself is presumed to be lawful: the test of unlawfulness lies in the purpose of the union.

A person becomes a member of a union by consenting to transfer a part of his own power over his own rights to the governing body of the union, which may be the general assembly or a committee of delegates. The legitimate power of the union over its members is in proportion to each member's power over his own actions—that is, to the quantity of the free-will of each

Chap. I. Common Law.

§ 1. *Formation and Force of Unions.*

member supposed to be transferred by him to the union; and the transfer is intended to relate, for the most part, to power over the money or the work of the individual member. The force acquired by combination is incalculably greater than the sum of the powers so transferred to the union by each individual, as is exemplified by soldiers for right, and by robbers for wrong. This multiplication of force by combining is a reason why combination for a purpose either of crime or of some classes of wrong is made criminal, the law prohibiting such combination having the expediency of checking wrong in its inception. At times, unions acquire power over both members and non-members by terrifying. Such power is in proportion to the terror; and terror for the most part decreases as knowledge of the extent of the danger, coupled with reliance on the law for protection, increases.

A union operates by way of agreement. If all its purposes should be free from unlawfulness, it would be like to a partnership agreement, for breach whereof the remedy is mostly in chancery; if any of its purposes should be unlawful, whether criminal or not, it would be so far void for illegality; if any of its purposes should be criminal, the concert would be a crime.

With respect to rights to property, they are not directly affected by the purposes of the

Chap. I. Common Law.

§ 1. *Formation and Force of Unions.*

owner of the property; but as unions operate by way of agreement, and as the validity of agreements depends on (among other things) the lawfulness of the purposes comprised in such agreement, the purposes of the unions may thus indirectly affect the rights of the members thereof to the joint property of the union. Accordingly, members of lawful unions have rights to the property of the union the same as other subjects to other joint property. Members of unions for unlawful purposes have no right to assistance from any court for the fulfilment of the unlawful purposes; but for all other purposes except the unlawful (if they can be distinctly severed) they are, I believe, in the same position as unions for lawful purposes.

Although these rights exist in law, it is difficult in practice to enforce them. In most unions the members are being changed perpetually by outgoing and incoming, while no provision has been made for transmission of rights of property; and probably no such provision could be effective without the aid of an Act of Parliament analogous to the Joint Stock Companies Acts. A remedy for violating a right of property cannot be enforced with certainty unless the owners of the right, when the alleged wrong was done, are ascertained.

As regards violations of the rights of property

CHAP. I. Common Law.

§ 1. *Formation and Force of Unions.*

belonging to the union done by members of the union—as, for example, by treasurers, clerks, and other such officers—there is the difficulty arising from the joint-ownership on the part of the wrongdoers. When the wrong is by the abstraction of property, neither trespass nor indictment can be maintained by the union against a member thereof for such abstraction. An attempt was made to remove this difficulty by section 44 of 18 and 19 Vict. c. 63 (the Friendly Societies Act), but this section has been found by experience not to afford a satisfactory remedy; and I venture to suggest that the law might be amended if it were enacted that a joint owner, under certain circumstances doing that which would be larceny or embezzlement as between him and the other joint owners, should be guilty notwithstanding his joint ownership. I see no reason why in the case of some societies, to be defined in the statute, a member taking or embezzling the goods of the society against the will of the other members, secretly with intent to deprive them of their right, and to change the property therein contrary to law, should not be made as responsible, civilly and criminally, as he would have been if no society had existed. If this was the law,[1] the trade unions would have

[1] Since this Memorandum was written, a statute to this effect (31 & 32 Vict. c. 116) has been passed, and under the statute a Treasurer of the Operative Bricklayers' Society has been con-

§ 1. *Formation and Force of Unions.*

the usual protection of the law against violation of rights of property by their own officers.

This protection might be supplemented by giving also to some societies a summary remedy analogous to the right given to friendly societies.

The test of unlawfulness is to be found in the purposes of the union. For example, if money is to be collected for the purpose of obtaining useful information, and regulating accordingly the supply of labour, the union is so far lawful; if the purpose is to apply its money to the injury of others—as, for instance, in burning the property or destroying the lives of persons obnoxious to the union—the union is so far unlawful. About such cases as these there is probably no dispute. But doubt about the lawfulness of the union arises when there is a purpose to restrain trade.

§ 2. *Right to Free Course for Trade in General.*

II. *Right to Free Course for Trade in General.*—Restraint of trade, according to a general principle of the common law, is unlawful. I say "a general principle," because the term "restraint of trade" is of very wide extension,

victed (R. *v.* Blackburn, C.C.C. Dec. 17, 1868). Now, therefore, unions have the aid of the criminal law against stealing; and if they remove illegality which is apparent on their rules they may, according to the decision in Farrer *v.* Close (see p. 79, *post*), have aid from the 44th section of the Friendly Societies' Act, 18 and 19 Vict. c. 63.

CHAP. I. Common Law.

§ 2. *Right to Free Course for Trade in General.*

and applies to a multitude of relations between man and man, relations which vary in countless permutation by the addition or subtraction of a circumstance; and the unlawfulness depends on the degree of restraint resulting from the circumstances. Questions of degree cannot be defined without a standard of measure: unlawful restraint of trade, therefore, cannot be defined, but it may be described; and the best description I can offer is this, that at common law every person has individually, and the public also have collectively, a right to require that the course of trade should be kept free from unreasonable obstruction.

Neither a grant of this right, nor a prohibition of the violation thereof, is found in the direct terms of a law; but proceedings for the violation of the right are recorded, and in these proceedings the grant of the right, and the prohibition of the violation thereof, are assumed to exist. The right to security for person and property is not granted affirmatively, but assaults and thefts are frequently subjects of recorded legal proceedings in which this right is assumed. The law has been described as *jubens honesta, prohibens contraria:* this may be true of written law, but in unwritten law the *jussum* is to be found in suits for violating the *prohibitum.*

CHAP. I. Common Law.

§ 2. *Right to Free Course for Trade in General.*

Many examples might be given of other rights to a free course in other matters which are known to the law not by express grant, but by enforcement of prohibition against violation thereof. The common law rights to a free course for passage on highways, or for light to the eyes, or for air to the lungs, or for the flow of the stream of water to the land of riparian proprietors, are not created by express grant, nor are they more capable of being perceived by any direct sense than the right to a free course for trade, there being no property either in any particle of light, or in air, or in running water, or in any passage on ways; but the existence of each of these rights is made known by actions or indictments for the infringement thereof. It may be worth adding, that the right to a free course for air or water is a right to quality as well as quantity. If either air or water is fouled in an unreasonable degree, action lies for a wrong in the class of nuisances; and the degree which is unreasonable is constantly shifting according as density of neighbourhood increases. These are examples of the application of the law relating to other nuisances, besides those relating to the free course for trade, in respect of air or water, light or passage, above referred to.

The right to a free course for trade is of great importance to commerce and productive

CHAP. I Common Law.

§ 2. *Right to Free Course for Trade in General.*

industry, and has been carefully maintained by those who have administered the common law during the time to which our records extend. The judgment of Parker, C.J., in Mitchel *v.* Reynolds (1 P. Williams, 181), is an authority showing the principle, and a limitation of it. The question was, whether a contract operating as a partial restraint of the trade of the vendor of the good-will of certain premises was valid; and the answer was in the affirmative, provided the restraint was not unreasonable with regard to the public interest, and not greater than was required for the interest of the purchaser (the party restraining), and provided also that the party restrained (the vendor) received value for that which he gave up. In that judgment previous cases showing restraint of trade to be illegal are examined, and the reasons for establishing the exceptive limitation are shown to be founded on the interests of truth and expediency. The report of this case in *Smith's Leading Cases* (vol. i. p. 356, 6th ed.), collects the principles of numerous decisions following Mitchel *v.* Reynolds, and defining more exactly the exceptive limitation.

The laws relating to fairs, markets, and staples; the prohibitions against forestalling, engrossing, regrating, monopolies, and all similar contrivances for affecting prices otherwise than by competition, have their origin in a purpose of keeping the course of trade free from obstruction, and enabling buyers and sellers to deal on the terms which free competition determines. These rules were made for the purpose of securing supply in times when stores were small, and transit difficult, and famine near if supply was delayed. Now, their utility, and therewith their operation, has nearly ceased under altered circumstances from the advance of civilization, it being found that supply is best secured by leaving mercantile speculation free. Accordingly, it was ruled by Lord Ellenborough in R. *v.* Cleasby (about the year 1812), that the engrossing of all the oil of a whaling season was no offence at common law in the then state of society; and he so held notwithstanding the case of R. *v.* Waddington, quoted below. The Legislature, by the 12 Geo. III. c. 71, repealed the statutes declaratory of the common law against engrossing; and the 7 & 8 Vict. c. 24, s. 1, enacts that no suit, civil or criminal, shall lie for engrossing. At the same time, by s. 4, the common law protection of the free course for trade against obstruction by means of falsehood is expressly continued. (See *Russell on Crimes*, by Greaves, b. ii., c. 19, vol. i., p. 252, 4th ed.)

§ 2. *Right to Free Course for Trade in General.*

A free course for trade has been carefully maintained from the earliest times. Lord Coke

CHAP. I. Common Law.

§ 2. *Right to Free Course for Trade in General.*

has collected some early authorities in his *Third Institute*, c. 89, on Forestalling. He goes back to the time of Ethelstan, and refers to laws in the time of that king, and also to laws in the time of the Conqueror, making provision for buying and selling in open market, by forbidding traffic above a certain value outside of a town unless with a witness. The clause in Magna Charta securing to each person his liberties is construed by him to include the right to a free course for trade possessed by the subjects of England (*Second Institute*, p. 47). There is also a conviction reported by him in the 43d Assize of Edward III., for affecting the market price of an article by spreading a false report.

To the authority of Lord Coke I would add a reference to the reports of some cases; and among them to Davenant *v.* Hurdis, in the time of Elizabeth (Moore, 576), deciding that a bye-law of the Merchant Taylors' Company, restricting the dressing of cloths to the freemen of the Company, was void for monopoly; and to the City of London's case (8 Co. 121 *b*), deciding that a charter from the King, granting that none but those free of the City should trade therein, was void for the same reason; also to the case of Monopolies (11 Co. 87*a*), where Lord Coke refers to a very ancient law, "You shall not take in pledge the nether and upper millstone, *quia animam suam apposuit tibi,"* (Deut. xxiv. 6) and says that by this it appears that every man's trade maintains his life, and that therefore he ought not to be deprived nor dispossessed of it any more than of his life. I would also refer to R. *v.* Waddington (1 East, 143), in the time of George III., where the defendant was convicted and punished for engrossing hops —that is, buying them wholesale with intent to sell them again wholesale. The arguments that were used by counsel and adopted by the Court in these cases, in support of the right to a free course for trade, show that the governing intention of those who administered the law was to promote the good of the community according to the light of their time, without partiality for any class, unless more scrupulous care for the protection of the less rich against the more rich class can be considered partiality. The intention of the judges in Waddington's case was in this sense entirely beneficent, although the prohibition there enforced against buying wholesale with intent to sell again wholesale has been since found under altered circumstances to be a mistake, as above explained.

§ 2. *Right to Free Course for Trade in General.*

III. *Right to Free Course for Trade in Labour.* —Under the general principle, operating upon all trade, which has been considered above, the

§ 3. *Right to Free Course for Trade in Labour.*

CHAP. I. Common Law.

§ 3. *Right to Free Course for Trade in Labour.*

law relating to freedom in disposing of either labour or capital, or both, is included. *Every person has a right under the law, as between him and his fellow subjects, to full freedom in disposing of his own labour or his own capital according to his own will. It follows that every other person is subject to the correlative duty arising therefrom, and is prohibited from any obstruction to the fullest exercise of this right which can be made compatible with the exercise of similar rights by others.* Every act causing an obstruction to another in the exercise of the right comprised within this description—done, not in the exercise of the actor's own right, but for the purpose of obstruction—would, if damage should be caused thereby to the party obstructed, be a violation of this prohibition; and the violation of this prohibition by a single person is a wrong, to be remedied either by action or by indictment, as the case may be. It is equally a wrong whether it be done by one or by many—subject to this observation, that a combination of many to do a wrong, in a matter where the public has an interest, is a substantive offence of conspiracy. It is equally a wrong, whether the obstruction be by means of an act unlawful in itself, on the part of the party obstructing, or by means of an act not otherwise unlawful.

§ 3. *Right to Free Course for Trade in Labour.*

Whether an act which does obstruct is unlawful seems to me to depend, under some circumstances, on the purpose of the actor: an example will help to explain my meaning. In R. *v.* Rowlands (5 Cox C. C. 436)[1] some of the defendants gave refreshment, or money, or advice to workmen going to the factory of Messrs. Perry, and thereby induced them to go away. The gift in each case might be for a purpose of beneficence towards the receiver, and might be lawful. But if it appeared that the refreshment produced incapacity, and the money paid the railway fare of a stupified man to an unknown place of concealment, and the persuasion deluded him into a railway carriage to be carried to that place, where he was to be abandoned, and if it further appeared that their absence brought ruin on Messrs. Perry, the justification on the ground of beneficent intention would be rebutted, and an act of obstruction done for the purpose of causing unjustified damage would remain proved, and would, in my opinion, be an act of unlawful obstruction which would render the parties to it liable to action or to indictment, as the case might be.

These propositions assume that a person has a right to do as he chooses with his own, whether labour or capital, within the limits set by

[1] See Appendix A, p. 81.

CHAP. I. Common Law.

§ 3. *Right to Free Course for Trade in Labour.*

law; that a right involves a prohibition against the infringement thereof; and that a prohibition involves a remedy for the violation thereof. If these propositions are sound, they may serve the purpose of giving a general notion of the direction of the law, and may be useful in suggesting the limits to which relaxation of restraint of trade ought to be carried. For effecting this purpose very wide propositions are pertinent. At the same time I am aware that such propositions assist but slightly in deciding specific cases of nuisance by obstruction, each of which involves for the most part many questions, of which I subjoin a few examples.

Rules relating to nuisance.

In the first place, it is a general rule relating to all nuisances, whether by obstruction or otherwise, that unlawfulness begins at a certain degree of annoyance, and that this degree is to be measured not by an exact standard, but on a supposed estimate of what is reasonable by men assumed to be prudent. In these words the defective nomenclature for legal ideas is exemplified, seeing that the terms "nuisance," "obstruction," "annoyance," may or may not denote unlawfulness. Secondly, the lawful exercise of a right is not a wrong. Where there are conflicting interests, the limits for the exercise of the rights relating to such interests vary as circumstances vary, and the adjustment of

§ 3. *Right to Free Course for Trade in Labour.*

the line where lawfulness ends and excess begins is not easy, because it is perpetually shifting. Each competitor in trade may hinder another, but the hindrance may not amount to unlawful obstruction. The process of adjustment of the line of lawfulness between rights which appear to conflict—the line where the exercise of a right is brought by excess to the confine of a wrong—is of continually increasing importance as a civilized population increases in density. The principle which guides in doing it cannot be conveniently explained here, but the subject is approached in the section (s. 6, p. 47), relating to the power of growth in the common law. Thirdly, the rights in respect of demand and supply of labour are in a sense reciprocal—that is, obstruction of supply must be an obstruction in the way of the demand, which would have been supplied but for the obstruction, and was not. Still there may be direct obstruction to the party supplying labour which may or may not be an obstruction to the party demanding it, according to the possibility of obtaining a supply elsewhere. Fourthly, the means of obstruction may be acts unlawful in themselves, but the intrinsic unlawfulness is irrelevant to their unlawfulness from obstructing the free course of trade. This proposition involves considerations of much complexity. I have above attempted to give one example of

Chap. I. Common Law.

§ 3. *Right to Free Course for Trade in Labour.*

my meaning, and I will only add a caution lest zeal for freedom to honest industry should result in giving facility to artful malignity. Fifthly, the obstruction may be caused by the use of words operating to alienate workmen or employers from each other. The use of such words for the purpose of obstructing trade may be either lawful or unlawful, upon the principles in accordance with which defamation injurious to character may be justifiable or not. Such defamation may be justified either for the protection of a lawful interest belonging to the defamer, or for the performance of a moral duty by him, provided always that the defamation be uttered without malice—that is, without a corrupt motive.

The application of these principles has caused endless discussion, but enough has been said in this place to exemplify the considerations involved in a legal proceeding for an alleged nuisance by obstruction of freedom to trade.

Objections answered. (Section V. p. 42.)

Objection has been made that the principles above laid down are not correct, being inconsistent with the restraints on barristers, physicians, and the like, and also with the restraints on employers and others under the Factory Acts. An answer to this is attempted in the section on this subject.

CHAP. I. Common Law.

§ 3. *Right to Free Course for Trade in Labour.*

Competition.

As to competition. It was said above that the question of unlawfulness arises when the transactions of the union are supposed to operate in restraint of trade: and when the action of the union is directed to the purpose either of raising wages in the case of working men, or of lowering wages in the case of employers, by any restraint upon freedom of competition, the question of unlawful restraint of trade has arisen. To this question the presumption is that the answer should be in the affirmative; but the answer cannot be certain unless the facts are specified, for this presumption may be rebutted by the circumstances, as is above suggested in reference to other alleged nuisances from obstruction.

Wages are said to rise and fall by the action of competition between labour and capital, and this may be true in ultimate results. But the competition to which the law for securing a free course for trade relates, is the competition between working men themselves where the supply of labour exceeds the demand, and between employers where the demand for labour of a given kind in a given locality exceeds the supply.

It seems inaccurate to describe the competition to be between the capitalist and the labourer; because the capitalist, in a stricter sense, is occupied in lending value at interest proportionate to risk, and is indifferent about wages

CHAP. I. Common Law.

§ 3. *Right to Free Course for Trade in Labour.*

and profits, production and prices. In a wider sense, many of the employed are owners of some capital in the shape of tools and other equipment. Many of the employers are borrowers only, and poorer than the employed; and the notion that employers are rich and powerful, and oppressive because they are employers, is unfounded.

Furthermore, it seems inaccurate to contradistinguish labourers or working men from capitalists or employers, as if they were separate classes; for both classes labour, and the labour of the brain for the employing class may be immeasurably more severe than the labour of the muscles of motion for the working class. All must labour by themselves or others, capital being past labour accumulated. The accumulated stores of the mental labour of past ages exceed in value all money. These stores must be used by the employer in the degree required by his business; but muscular action may be supplied with very slight recourse to accumulated knowledge in many departments of labour. There is no hardship in labour, unless excessive; it is the condition for the existence of happiness universally, and in moderation is a grand boon.

It is also true, in one sense, that all employed are employers, and all employers are employed, according to the relation of the person in respect of whom the term is applied to some other person with whom he is compared.

Chap. I. Common Law.

§ 3. *Right to Free Course for Trade in Labour.*

I do not advert further to competition between classes, because the law is concerned directly with the rights of individuals, and only indirectly with the interests of classes, and because the free course for trade secured by law is a free course for each individual to dispose of his labour or his capital according to his own choice. Moreover, the attempt to restrain trade in the relation between employers and employed begins for the most part with attempts in the way of combination, whereby the individuals of one class, either employers or labourers, attempt to restrain others of the same class from direct competition with themselves. Up to a certain point the attempt may be lawful. The question is thus raised, What is the point at which the attempt begins to be unlawful? And the answer, I submit, should be—When unlawful coercion is attempted to be put upon the will of any individual in disposing of his labour or his capital.

Unlawful Obstruction of Trade.

It is not easy to give a definition which shall include every kind of "unlawful coercion:" but it seems clear that the causing of damage to the person or the property or the estimation of the party to be coerced, either by unlawful action, or by falsehood (including all deception),

Chap. I. Common Law.

§ 3. *Right to Free Course for Trade in Labour.*

or by causing the fear of such damage from unlawful action or falsehood, or by obstructing the party who is to be coerced in the exercise of any right connected with trade by unlawful action or by falsehood—for the purpose of swaying or defeating his will in disposing of his labour or his capital—would be instances of unlawful coercion, and so of unlawful restraint of trade.

I submit that there may also be unlawful obstruction to the free course of trade without any such unlawful coercion as is above described. Restraint of the free course for trade in labour by acts of molestation or obstruction, which are not otherwise unlawful, but which operate as a hindrance to the exercise of a trade, and which are done for the purpose of such hindrance without justification, seems to me, as above stated, to be an actionable wrong. The Act 6 Geo. IV. c. 129 is, in my opinion, declaratory of the common law as to the offence, and operative only to make a summary remedy. The statute declares acts of molestation or obstruction, as well as acts of violence, intimidation, and threats, to be an offence: but of this more when we come to the statutes.

Furthermore, I think that there may also be unlawful restraint of trade without coercion by unlawful means, and without such obstruction or molestation as is last above mentioned.

Chap. I. Common Law.

§ 3. *Right to Free Course for Trade in Labour.*

I assume that the employer and the employed have each a right to a free course for trade in labour, as above described. The supply of labour to the employer is stopped if the working-man chooses to stop; and assuming for the present that his act is lawful whenever he freely chooses so to do, still a party who induces him so to do may, in so doing (as it seems to me) infringe the right of the employer to a free course for the supply of labour. I take the case of money paid to the working-man to induce him to stop, in which the motive for so paying is malice towards the employer—that is, some corrupt or spiteful motive. I put aside money so paid from a motive of supposed interest, as in the case of some strikes, and assume it to be paid for the sole purpose of ruining the employer or destroying his manufacture. A question is thus raised, Does the law allow it? I think not. A stop in the supply of labour is obviously a damage in every trade; the causing of the stop is a restraint of trade; and all restraint of trade is, as above stated, presumed to be unlawful until the contrary be shown. Such a stop may be lawful, as for instance, where the money is paid by a competitor offering higher wages to obtain workmen; but in the case supposed the money is paid "not to work" for a particular party, for the sole purpose of causing

Chap. I. Common Law.

§ 3. *Right to Free Course for Trade in Labour.*

damage to that party whose supply is thus stopped. If the party paying for such a stop attempts to rebut the presumption of unlawfulness by alleging an honest purpose, the question of motive is the issue; and if the motive is found to be malicious, it seems to me to accord with principle that he should be found guilty of a wrong and made liable to damages. If two or more combined for the purpose of so causing damage, the combination would, I believe, be a crime. Other cases may be put of a wrong inflicted by paying money for the purpose of buying absence in order to cause damage to a third party. If a person would be material as a witness in an approaching trial, would it not be a wrongful obstruction to the course of justice for the adverse party to pay him to conceal himself so that he could not be summoned to attend, although no duty to attend would be created before service of a summons? And so, before the statutes against corrupt practices at elections, would not an action have lain for paying a voter to be out of the way at polling-time?

What has been said of gifts of money for the purpose of stopping supply of labour is true, *mutatis mutandis*, of persuasion for the same purpose.

The law relating to comments on the conduct

§ 3. Right to Free Course for Trade in Labour.

of men in public capacities affords an analogy. Such comments, however defamatory, are justified, if the motive of the writer be not corrupt: but if a private enemy of such a man were to hire a defaming writer to write him down, and such a hiring was in proof, the motive would be corrupt, and the justification would fail; and any of the parties to such defamation would be liable in an action for damages. So he who attempts to justify a stop in the supply of labour to another, by persuading workmen to leave him for the sole purpose of gratifying his spite against the employer, ought to be made liable—and, I believe, is liable at common law—for the damage caused by such persuasion.

This is enough to indicate my opinion as to the effect of the common law prohibition against restraint upon trade in labour either by unlawful coercion or, in some instances, by other means.

Combination.

As to combination, each person has a right to choose whether he will labour or not, and also to choose the terms on which he will consent to labour, if labour be his choice. The power of choice in respect of labour and terms, which one person may exercise and declare singly, many after consultation may exercise jointly, and they may make a simultaneous declaration of their

CHAP. I. Common Law.

§ 3. *Right to Free Course for Trade in Labour.*

choice, and may lawfully act thereon for the immediate purpose of obtaining the required terms; but they cannot create any mutual obligation having the legal effect of binding each other not to work or not to employ unless upon terms allowed by the combination. Any arrangement for that purpose, whatever may be its purport or form, does not bind as an agreement, but is illegal, though not unlawful, on account of restraint of trade, and therefore void. Every party to it, who chooses to put an end to it, is thenceforward as free to claim his own terms for his own labour as if such arrangement had never been made; and any attempt to enforce, by unlawful coercion, performance of any such supposed agreement, against a party who chooses to break from it and labour or contract for labour upon different terms, is an attempt to obstruct him in the lawful exercise of his right to freedom to trade; and is thus a private wrong. It is also a violation of a duty towards the public—that is to say, of the duty to abstain from obstructing the exercise of the right to the free course of trade. A person can neither alienate for a time his freedom to dispose of his own labour or his own capital according to his own will (see Hilton *v.* Eckersley, 6 Ell. & Bl. 47), nor alienate such freedom generally and make himself a slave (see the argument of Hargrave in the Negro Sommersett's case, 20 State Trials, 23); it follows that he cannot transfer it to the governing body of a union.

§ 3. *Right to Free Course for Trade in Labour.*

The reported cases exemplifying the application of these principles of common law are not numerous, because for some centuries statutes were passed with the intent of regulating the rate of wages, and the mode of conducting business, by the interference of the magistrate. But the law of this subject was much debated in Hilton *v.* Eckersley in the Queen's Bench and in the Exchequer Chamber; and the inalienability of the right to freedom in disposing of labour or capital according to the will of the individual owner was there affirmed.

Hilton v. *Eckersley.*

In that case several employers had mutually bound themselves under a penalty to carry on their respective concerns according to the will of the majority. The bond was held void for restraint of trade; and the opinion of Erle, J., to the effect that capitalists had the same rights in respect of capital as working men had in respect of labour, and that working men had *a right* to make any agreement for transferring to others the disposal of their labour which they chose (meaning an agreement of binding force) for the purpose of raising wages, was held to

Chap. I. Common Law.

§ 3. *Right to Free Course for Trade in Labour.*

be wrong. It follows that expressions to the same effect supposed to have been used by him in R. *v.* Rowlands and R. *v.* Duffield (5 Cox C.C. 436 and 404) were also incorrect. These expressions seem to have been founded on a misconstruction of the 6 Geo. IV. c. 129, s. 4; whereas, although by that section it was enacted that combinations and agreements for raising or lowering wages should be exempted from criminal responsibility, yet they were not made lawful.[1] The cases of R. *v.* Rowlands and R. *v.* Duffield are noticed in the Appendix.

R. v *Rowlands, and R.* v. *Duffield.* (*Appendix A, p.* 1.)

These are the general principles in accordance with which unreasonable restraint of trade in disposing of labour or capital is prohibited, and freedom in disposing thereof is maintained. The practical application of these principles lies in indictment for violation of duty towards the public, and in action for violation of a private right, according to the circumstances of the case in which a remedy for a wrong is sought.

I do not attempt to follow the application of these principles to supposed cases any farther, on account of the difficulty of com-

1 A judgment for the plaintiff in Hilton *v.* Eckersley might probably have been supported on the ground that the circumstances of society which gave occasion for some of the rules of the common law and many of the statutes against combinations of working men were changed, the common law being in a state of perpetual growth: *cessante ratione, cessat lex.* The law is as the judges declare it to be.

§ 3. Right to Free Course for Trade in Labour.

prising all the relevant facts in the supposition. Men having the qualities requisite for dealing with legal principles—that is, who are qualified to assist either in administering the law as attorneys, advocates, or judges, or in amending the law as legislative advisers—would, I expect, have power to apply them. The requisite qualities are—

First, a general knowledge of the body of the law in its organic entirety, by which the relation of each part to the living body is perceived, in analogy with which the relation of a living branch to its parent tree is understood. For example, if action lies, there must have been a right and a violation of it—that is, a wrong; if indictment lies, there must have been a duty towards the public and a breach thereof.

Secondly, a capacity for extracting principles from adjudications, and raising them by abstraction to a wide extension, and afterwards perceiving their effect pervading subordinate principles.

And thirdly, sagacity in taking from the multitude of facts which must be always coexisting at the time and place when and where a complainant alleges he was wronged, the facts relevant to show the right and the violation thereof, and also the facts relevant to show the limitation of the supposed right within the degree

CHAP. I. Common Law.

§ 3. *Right to Free Course for Trade in Labour.*

which prudent men consider reasonable; and after this process rejecting the rest as immaterial.

To the consideration of men who possess these qualifications this statement of principles is offered, for the purpose not of specific adjudication but of future legislation.

The interests of men of industry are deeply involved in the existence of these principles, and their interest is protected by the law equally with other interests. Their opinions of their interest are important as evidence of the existence of such interests; but let me add that the opinion of such men, if unused to legal reasoning, upon the soundness of any principle of law, is not of the same importance. There are unnumbered persons in every rank of life enjoying the benefits resulting from innumerable principles of law which they understand imperfectly, and to which they could not give expression.

§ 4. *Proceedings for Violation of the Right to Freedom in Trade.*

(a) *Action for civil wrongs.*

(b) *Indictment for criminal wrongs other than conspiracy.*

IV. *Proceedings for Violation of the Right to Freedom for the Course of Trade.*—The remedies under the common law, for obstruction to the free course of trade, are either by action for private wrongs or by prosecution for criminal offences. I do not find any reported cases showing that resort has been had to proceedings for the civil injury which would

§ 4. *Proceedings for Violation of the Right to Freedom in Trade.*

throw light on the present inquiry; and as to criminal offences, since the crime is almost always committed by a combination, the remedy by indictment for conspiracy has been most usual, as in practice it has been found most convenient.

Still, if there be any such private right to freedom for the course of trade as is above described, it follows that an action lies for a violation of that right; and if there be a duty towards the public to keep the course of trade free from obstruction, indictment would lie for breach of that duty. It is clear that action lies for causing loss of service by enticing away servants from their hiring; and by analogy there should be a remedy for preventing hiring by obstructing for a malicious purpose the free course for the supply of labour. If the same reasoning be correct, an indictment might be sustained against a single person in some cases for obstructing the free course of trade. But the law of conspiracy applied to restraint of trade is the more usual remedy, and is therefore of more practical importance. And before entering on it, it may be worth while to notice briefly a distinction between a civil injury and a criminal wrong.

Distinction between civil and criminal wrongs.

A civil injury is for the most part complete when the external act has been done which violates a right and causes damage, and it is not

Chap. I. Common Law.

§ 4. *Proceedings for Violation of the Right to Freedom in Trade.*

necessary to inquire into the intention with which that act was done, unless want of malice should be admissible as a defence, in which case the malicious intent may become material in reply. But a crime cannot be completed by muscular action alone: there must always be in addition a criminal intention, in respect either of commission or omission, and the criminal intention is an essential element of criminality; the external act being material for the purpose of evidencing the criminal intention, as well as to bring the matter within the scope of human law, which does not pass upon bare intention without an illegal act, or an attempt to commit such act, or a conspiracy. Every act that can be adduced as the sign of a criminal intention is consistent with many intentions, some criminal, some not; so that the inquiry in a criminal case, after identifying the actor and the act, is always a question of intention. For example, where a chattel has been moved, it may be with intent to exercise a right, or with intent to steal; so also, where a latch is lifted, it may be by a friend coming to visit or by a felon coming to steal; so also, where an incision has been made, it may be with intent to cure by a surgeon, or with intent to kill by a murderer: the criminality of the act depends on the intention with which it was accompanied. The external act of supposed criminality in some crimes may consist of words only, and in that case the evidence of the words is evidence of the intention; words, where they have a clear meaning, being as directly indicative of intention as actions. High treason has been at times proved by proof of words passing in a consultation of conspirators against the king. So, also, charges of conspiracy as a misdemeanour, with intention either to restrain trade or to do other wrong, may be proved by words only of mutual agreement, if they clearly show the criminal intention.

CHAP. I. Common Law.

§ 4. Proceedings for Violation of the Right to Freedom in Trade.

Conspiracy in general.

With respect to the crimes classed under the term "conspiracy," the external act of the crime is concert, by which mutual consent to a common purpose is exchanged. The test of the criminality of the concert lies in the intent or purpose of the concert.

All crimes are wrongs, either against persons or the public; and it is undisputed law that a combination for the purpose of committing a crime is a crime. All rights are created by law, and violations of rights are wrongs, and some wrongs are crimes; but the quality of guilt which makes a wrong to be a crime is known only by practice, and has not been defined in apt words, as is above stated. The public, correctly speaking, has no capacity for a right,

CHAP. I. Common Law.

§ 4. *Proceedings for Violation of the Right to Freedom in Trade.*

not being a person; but there are duties towards the public of great importance, and it is convenient to speak of the public having rights correlating with those duties. Adopting this form of speaking, it may be said that wrongs become crimes by reference to the importance of the public right violated thereby; but whatever be the essence of crime, it is certain that a combination to commit a crime is a crime.

De Berenger's case.

There seems also to be authority for saying that a combination to violate a private right, in which the public has a sufficient interest, is a crime, such a violation being an actionable wrong. De Berenger's case (3 M. & S. 67), if I understand it aright, is an example. He combined with others to spread at the Stock Exchange a false report of the death of Buonaparte, for the purpose of raising the price of stocks and selling at the rise. In my opinion, he violated by the use of falsehood the private right of the purchasers in the market to buy at the price settled by competition; and the Court decided that the public has an interest in the security of the public funds sufficient to make such a combination to effect a private wrong a crime. The limitation excluding from this category of crimes the class of injuries in which the public has not a sufficient interest appears from the case of R. *v.* Turner (13 East, 228), deciding that a combination for

R. v. Turner.

§ 4. *Proceedings for Violation of the Right to Freedom in Trade.*

the purpose of taking hares unlawfully is not indictable for that reason; and this limitation is sanctioned by Lord Campbell in Hilton *v.* Eckersley (6 Ell. & Bl. 47), by his saying "that the decision was wrong in respect of fact, for it appeared in the statement of the facts that the defendants were armed to resist the owner of the hares, and that it was therefore a combination for the purpose of a breach of the peace, and for that reason a crime." This correction of the judgment in respect of fact is an implied assent to its correctness in point of law if the facts had been as they were assumed to be. A combination for wrong gives facilities to wrongdoers, as above stated; so that a combination to trespass may with reason be held to be a crime, although the trespasser, if single, would be liable to action only and not to indictment.

There are other cases of conspiracy not so specially defined.

The guilt of conspiracy may arise from simultaneity of action which an individual could not incur by himself, as a combination of a crowd for the purpose of so using a highway as to do harm to other passengers.

There are also public interests of great importance in respect of which some combinations for the purpose of violating the public rights therein are crimes, although such violations by

Chap. I. Common Law.

§ 4. *Proceedings for Violation of the Right to Freedom in Trade.*

an individual alone may not be always indictable. Justice, morality, polity, and trade are examples of such public interests.

Combinations to pervert justice by deception are criminal; and the statute of Edward I. against conspiracies to maintain false pleas is declaratory of the common law on that subject.

R. v. Mawbey.

R. *v.* Mawbey (6 T. R. 619) is an example of this crime, where the defendants (two justices) combined for the purpose of deceiving the Quarter Sessions by a false certificate of road repair.

As to morality, the law coincides therewith, although it does not vindicate every breach thereof; and there is a class of cases where the interference of the law is supported on the ground of morality. In this class are the combinations for deluding women into unchastity, either by aggravated seduction (see R. *v.* Lord Grey, 9 State Trials, 127), or by deceptive forms of marriage (see the cases collected in *Russell on Crimes*, by Greaves, b. v. c. 2, vol. iii. pp. 130 *et seq.* 4th ed.). In this class also is included the case of R. *v.* Delaval and others (3 Burr. 1435), where the defendant Delaval combined with the master of a girl apprenticed to learn singing to take an assignment of her apprenticeship for the purpose of teaching and seducing her, and they were convicted of conspiracy. The ground of the decision is not given, as no objection was

CHAP. I. Common Law.

§ 4. *Proceedings for Violation of the Right to Freedom in Trade.*

made. But it cannot be disputed that such conduct was a breach of the duty created by an ordinary deed of apprenticeship towards the apprentice and her parents, and so a personal wrong and a civil injury. It was also a violation of the public interest in the chastity of the women who are inclined to be chaste, to make the rights conferred by law on masters subserve the purpose of doing this wrong to an apprentice.

The combinations for seditious purposes are violations of the public interest in maintaining the polity established by law. Of these cases no explanation is required.

Conspiracies connected with Trade.

I come now to conspiracies connected with trade.

Some of the laws which affect the distribution of commodities, and make provision in order that supply and demand may meet and deal upon the terms obtained by free competition, have been above referred to.

The laws affecting the production of commodities make similar provision, *mutatis mutandis*, in order that all the parties concerned in the process required for the production of a saleable product may deal as to labour upon the terms obtained by free competition. Such obstruction as is above described to free competition in

CHAP. I. Common Law.

§ 4. *Proceedings for Violation of the Right to Freedom in Trade.*

disposing of labour or capital is an unlawful restraint of trade, and a combination so to restrain trade by preventing free competition is the crime of conspiracy, being a violation of a private right in which the public has an interest, and also a violation of a duty towards the public.

It seems essential that the terms obtained by free competition should prevail consistently throughout all the processes involved in production, seeing that it is commercially useless if it will not fetch a remunerative price after paying the cost of production, the amount of which cost depends on the terms obtained by competition.

The employer has to go through many processes of cost and risk: he has to deal with the landlord for premises, with the capitalist for money and fixed capital, and with artisans for work. The employed has to take the wages for which he consents to work without the same risk or cost. In all these processes the law provides for the action of free competition, making a combination in restraint of trade by so obstructing free competition, as is above described, the crime of conspiracy.

In relation to production the combinations of the employed to obstruct free competition amongst the working class for wages are more frequent than combinations of employers to obstruct free competition amongst themselves.

Chap. I. Common Law.

§ 4. *Proceedings for Violation of the Right to Freedom in Trade.*

The interest of the employed in a uniform rate of wages is more common to the class in general than the interest of the employers in any attempt to make a uniform scale of prices or profits. Moreover, the employed are a more numerous class, and by reason of closer companionship in factories and the like, and more constant interchange of mind there, have more facilities for acting in concert. These considerations may account for more frequent proceedings against working men than against employers, without imputing partiality in the administration of the law.

(c) Indictment for conspiracy.

The tendency to combine for the purpose of raising or lowering wages appears from the manifold statutes passed for the purpose of adjusting a current rate of wages on some basis other than free competition. These statutes have long since been repealed. While they were in force they tended to prevent a resort to the common law remedy for conspiracy, and the records of proceedings under the common law against conspirators for the purpose of restraining freedom for labour are not numerous; but still there are authorities sufficient to show what the law is in this matter.

In the collections of precedents for indictments for conspiracy to raise wages, in violation

CHAP. I. Common Law.

§ 4. *Proceedings for Violation of the Right to Freedom in Trade.*

Hilton v. *Eckersley.*

of the statutes fixing a maximum, which are given in Wentworth and Chitty, there are counts for combining not to work for less than the required wages, founded on the common law prohibition against restraint of trade; but the most important authority is Hilton *v.* Eckersley (6 Ell. & Bl. 47) before mentioned. There an agreement by employers to carry on business as the majority should direct was decided to be in restraint of trade at common law, and illegal and void, though exempt from prosecution under 6 George IV. c. 129, as mentioned above. The case is cited here for the sake of the judgment of Crompton, J., who held that such an agreement would be "indictable at common law, as tending directly to impede and interfere with the free course of trade and manufacture," and to take away "the freedom of action of an individual to carry on his trade...... according as it may be for his interest or that of the public." He dwelt also on the mischief that would follow if parties should give up the right of judging for themselves, and place themselves under the dictation either of a majority or of a committee of delegates. Crompton, J. was remarkable for learning, depth, and acuteness, and was painfully conscientious about speaking accurately when he spoke judicially. I believe also that he never recognised the notion that the common law

Chap. I. Common Law.

§ 4. *Proceedings for Violation of the Right to Freedom in Trade.*

adapts itself by a perpetual process of growth to the perpetual roll of the tide of circumstances as society advances. His judgment in this case is direct to the point that an agreement for any coercion whatever, restraining the free-will of each party by the will of the whole, is an illegal restraint of trade, and indictable at common law. Other judges held the bond to be illegal, but reserved their opinion on the point of criminality. Erle, J. held it to be legal; and his opinion was adjudged to be wrong, as above mentioned.

Walsby v. Anley.

Walsby *v.* Anley (30 L. J. M. C. 121) is also a decision bearing on this point. Walsby combined with other workmen to leave the employ of Anley simultaneously, unless he discharged certain workmen who were working under a declaration which they objected to. They thus conspired to coerce his will in the exercise of his right to a free course of trade in respect of hiring and discharging. Crompton and Hill, J.J. held that this was a conspiracy indictable at common law. The question was raised by an appeal against a conviction for endeavouring by threats to force the employer to limit the number of his workmen, under 6 Geo. IV. c. 129, s. 3. The words of alleged threat were: "Unless the men who are working under the declaration be discharged, we cease to work immediately."

Chap. I. Common Law.

§ 4. *Proceedings for Violation of the Right to Freedom in Trade.*

The objection to the conviction was, that this was no threat, because each had a right to leave singly, and it was contended that it followed that all had a right to leave simultaneously. The objection was overruled by all the judges, but on different grounds; by the Chief Justice on the ground that a notice of an intended simultaneous stop of work, with the prohibited intent, was a criminal threat within the statute. But I cite the case here for the sake of the judgments of Crompton and Hill, J.J., who held that the threat must be of an illegal act, and that a combination for a simultaneous stop of work for the purpose of annoying the master was an obstruction to the free course of trade, and a crime; and Crompton, J. refers to his judgment in Hilton *v.* Eckersley, and affirms its correctness, notwithstanding the objections thereto by Mr. Longe in his pamphlet on the *Law of Strikes.*[1] It should be noted that the simultaneity of the leaving makes the damage, and that the act of one cannot cause that damage.

R. v. Mawbey.

The dictum of Grose, J. in R. *v.* Mawbey (6 T. R. 636), relating to the criminality of combinations to raise wages, was relevant only for the purpose of establishing that the guilt of conspiracy is complete by the agreement.

[1] *An Inquiry into the Law of Strikes.* By F. D. Longe. Cambridge and London, 1860.

The case had no connexion with wages, as explained above.

Chap. I. Common Law.

§ 4. *Proceedings for Violation of the Right to Freedom in Trade.*

R. v. Journeymen Tailors of Cambridge.

In R. *v.* Journeymen Tailors of Cambridge (8 Mod. 10) the conspiracy was to refuse to work at a less sum per day than was demanded, being at a higher rate than the maximum of wages fixed under the statute 5 Eliz. c. 4.

The dicta in the last two cases, that acts lawful for one may become indictable if more than one combine to commit them, were not pertinent to the adjudication then being made. The judges do not refer to examples, and although the proposition may be true of cases where simultaneity is the essence of the criminality of the act, I cannot discover any other cases in which it would be true.

From the authorities referred to it appears that the crime of conspiracy consists of two elements—namely, an intention, and an agreement by two or more to execute it; that an intention to use such coercion as is above described to be unlawful, against any person in the exercise of his right to freedom to trade, is sufficient as to one element of conspiracy; and that the making of the agreement to execute the intention completes the offence. The mere intention, without some act equivalent to an attempt to execute it, is not sufficient, but the outward act by which mutual consent to an agreement is interchanged is sufficient to complete the offence.

CHAP. I. Common Law.

§ 4. *Proceedings for Violation of the Right to Freedom in Trade.*

If this reasoning is correct, the common law in force since the statute of 6 George IV. secures to every person freedom to follow his own will as to working and employment, and also as to combining with others in respect of wages and hours, and for all other lawful purposes; but he has no right to use unlawful means, either by himself or in combination with others, in order to coerce the will of another party to prevent him from working or employing as he may choose; and probably he has no right to apply the power of a combination for the purpose either of malicious damage or of unjust extortion, although he uses no unlawful means except combining to obstruct the free course of trade, in order to effect such purpose.

§ 5. *Statutable and Professional Restraints of Freedom to Labour.*

V. *Statutable and Professional Restraints of Freedom to Labour.*—Two objections have been offered to the correctness of the principle that every employer and every working man has a right, as between him and his fellow subjects, to act according to his own will in disposing of his own capital or his own labour as far as is compatible with the rights of others: first, because the law has put several restraints upon this freedom; and secondly, because in the professions of a physician and an advocate usage has put some restraints on this freedom in regard to the amount of fees.

Chap. I. Common Law.

§ 5. *Statutable and Professional Restraints of Freedom to Labour.*

(a) Restraints by law, as by Factory Acts.

As to the first objection, one answer is contained in the words used in defining the principle, by which its application is limited to the right of one subject *as against another subject.*

All rights are created by law, and are regulated by law: the right to the freedom as above described, although protected from violation by other subjects, is still regulated under the law. The law restrains the working man of every rank from many kinds of work unless he has a legal qualification. He may not work in certain medical, legal, military, and nautical capacities, unless qualified according to law. These are examples of restraints imposed by law to save the public from damage by reason of want of skill. There are also restraints imposed by law to save the party restrained from damage by reason of his own ignorance or helplessness, such as restraints on women and children from excess of labour under the Factory Acts, or restraints on working men in some deleterious trades from sacrifice of health. Restraints also from trade unless qualified by apprenticeship are restraints under the law. So the law restrains the capitalist from disposing of his capital for purposes which violate legality, morality, public policy, and the like. Restraints may also be imposed by law on parties incapable from infancy or mental disease of managing their own affairs for their own sake.

CHAP. I. Common Law.

§ 5. Statutable and Professional Restraints of Freedom to Labour.

These restraints by law are distinct from restraints by the will of another subject. The fullest freedom under the law as between him and his fellow subjects is compatible with countless restraints imposed by law for the benefit of his fellow subjects individually, or of the public generally, or of himself. The right to this freedom for the capitalist and the working man is part of the right to property and personal security, and is subject to analogous restraints. It is analogous to the right to passage according to will on a highway: generally speaking, all have it; but an individual may be restrained by lawful imprisonment, and all may be restrained when the law authorises a stop of passage. Some unions attempt to restrain the freedom of the members either without authority of law, as by agreements which are void, because contrary to public policy; or in violation of law, as where rules in restraint of trade are enforced by unlawful means. There is no analogy between these restraints and such restraints under the law as are above mentioned.

(b) Professional fees.

The second objection, founded on the usage relating to the fees for physicians and advocates, has been applied both for the purpose of impeaching the principle of freedom for the course of trade, and for the purpose of justifying the action of those unions which fix a

§ 5. *Statutable and Professional Restraints of Freedom to Labour.*

minimum wage for an artisan; but whatever be the purpose for which the objection is used, it seems to be founded on a misconception, and to be irrelevant to the law relating to trade unions.

The action of unions, so far as it excludes non-unionists from work, and requires for unionists wages to a certain amount, is founded on a supposed monopoly of a given kind of work in a given district. All such work is assumed to be the property of the union: if all the workmen who can supply the work are in the union, the monopoly is secured; and the usual action has been to increase wages and decrease work until a maximum amount of wages has been extracted from the employers, and the equal distribution of the minimum amount of work secured for each member.

This action has no analogy to the usage of the two professions above named. The exclusion of unqualified men from practice is not for the sake of giving a monopoly of practice to the qualified, as explained above. It is not in order to limit number, but to secure efficiency. Neither have the physicians or barristers any combined action for extracting from patients or suitors the maximum of money for the minimum of work, and distributing it equally among all the members of those two profes-

§ 5. Statutable and Professional Restraints of Freedom to Labour.

sions. It is clear that the usual amount of a professional fee is settled on a different principle from that which regulates the wages for service. In these two professions service is in law gratuitous, and is often so in fact. It cannot be estimated at any market rate: the external act of service may be almost imperceptible, indeed it may lie in a word; and yet the value of it to the recipient may be immeasurably great. Probably bargaining in each case would be unpleasant to both parties, and a settlement by custom is preferred. Whatever may be the reason for the usage, enough has been said to show that it is founded on a principle different from that by which unions seek to regulate wages. I would only add a reference to Kennedy *v.* Broun et ux. (32 L. J., N. S., C. P. 137), where the right of an advocate to sue for remuneration was negatived: the reason given for the adjudication accords with this explanation.

If it should appear to any that a party making a contract for his labour is coerced if the opposite party require him either to perform his contract, or to pay damages for the breach of it, it would not be superfluous to remark that freedom to dispose of labour consists in freedom to contract for disposing of it. Labour, unless gratuitous, can only be disposed of by hire, so that a contract for hire is an application of the principle, not an exception from it: restraint arises when the party is restrained from using his own will in making a contract for his own labour.

§ 5. Statutable and Professional Restraints of Freedom to Labour.

The same observation is true of any restraint supposed to be created by partnership. The restraint on property is created by an assignment of private property to the partnership; and the restraint on service, if any, is created by the contract for agency involved in the contract of partnership.

§ 6. The Roots and Growth of the Common Law.

VI. *The Roots and Growth of the Common Law.*—There are some relations between man and man which do not change, such as birth; and the rules of law relating thereto do not change. There are other relations which are perpetually changing as society progresses, and the conflicts of rights caused by this perpetual process of change is the subject of a perpetual process of adjustment, according to principles contained in the common law. The serfs and copyholders of the middle ages passed through many variations of rights, as well at common law as by statute, before they became enfranchised electors.

Rights in respect of contracts, restraint of trade, combination, the relation between em-

CHAP. I. Common Law.

§ 6. *The Roots and Growth of the Common Law.*

ployer and employed, and some kinds of nuisances, afford examples of perpetual change. An attempt to adjust them by statute may succeed, if the authors and interpreters of the statute understand the principles of the common law, and in some degree incorporate them. Without that process the interpretation of the words of a statute merely by a dictionary leads often to unsatisfactory results. Even if the statute is well drawn, society soon progresses beyond it, and the need of the principles of the common law is constantly renewed.

I therefore offer a few words on the power of growth in the common law. I do so with misgiving, having no judicial authority for my opinion that I know of.

Every rule of the common law ought to be applied with some limitation of reasonableness in degree. The relations of ideas of number, measure, and weight may be expressed in unlimited terms with absolute certainty; but it is not so with the relations of the actions of man upon man. Those relations cannot be defined till the laws of matter, and also the laws of mind, are within the limits of certain knowledge, and till social progress is stopped. Definite rules therefore may not be expected. In the meantime life multiplies, proximity increases, and each man would become a nuisance to his neighbour in respect (among manifold other matters) of air and water, labour and capital, production and distribution, if a perpetual process of adjustment was not in constant action. This adjustment is effected by the principles of the Common Law.

§ 6. *The Roots and Growth of the Common Law.*

These principles originate practically from the people. Proximity leads to mutual help in a known course of business; a known course of business involves the recognition of some established principles. These principles may be acted on long before a complete language is framed. A course of business without a verbal law is equivalent to living law; a verbal law not in accordance with the course of business cannot be practically enforced.

In all assemblies of free men each man has authority in proportion as his mind is noble. The test of nature's nobility is industry. In agriculture, trade, and manufacture, the men of most influence are in effect seers, and the seers establish the course of business which is considered by them the most expedient at the time; and in case of dispute the same seers are trusted as arbitrators to apply the principles involved in the course of business. The principles are applied at first in the concrete; gradually they grow into rules of wider application, and words grow appropriate for their

Chap. I. Common Law.

§ 6. *The Roots and Growth of the Common Law.*

expression; and the judiciary men and the legislative men adopt them. Throughout this process the rules practically originate from the people.[1] In a mass of free people the unsophisticated majority, according to experience, are certain to intend to side with the kind and true against the false and malicious: the compound of the kind and true being the just.

This process has in all mercantile countries been in constant action, as the law merchant is in its theory adjusted by the usage of merchants. The same process was in constant action in the Saxon county-courts presided over by the sheriff. The *probi et legales homines* attending on the county-court were men of practical business engaged in useful industry, and living in the neighbourhood. From them the jurymen were selected; and the jury so taken were judges both of the law and of the fact, the sheriff having power to keep order on the trial, but having no power to guide the decision. The law must therefore have been found by the jury in the traditions of the course of the business in which the contention arose, and in their own sense of right.

So far as rules of conduct for practical people are concerned, it matters not whether justice is

[1] See Savigny's *Traité de Droit romain*, translated by Guenoux, lib. i. cap. 2, ss. 7 and 9, *Droit populaire.*

supposed to have its source in inductive search after utility, or in an intuitive perception of right to be tested by utility, inasmuch as utility and right in this sense lead to a similar course of action. One man obeys conscience tested by utility; another takes utility alone for a guide.

Chap. I. Common Law.

§ 6. *The Roots and Growth of the Common Law.*

But if the origin of the principles of the common law is to be traced beyond their practical existence, they seem to originate from conscience—that is, from the same power which has made the majority of all free men of all ages and languages to have a perception of that which they feel to be just, and which they admire for itself, and assume to be useful till the contrary be proved. And among such free men some are pre-eminently gifted with this perception of the just.

The jurists whose words are recorded in the civil law rely on their own sense of right where an opinion is adopted because "*æquum esse mihi videtur.*" The words of these men would not have been handed down if they had merely expressed their intuitions before their highest faculties had been trained by long and painful efforts both to understand the relations of man to man, and the words of wide extension expressive of those relations, and also to know how far those relations had been so adjusted by the men who had gone before as that their adjustment had

CHAP. I
Common Law.

§6. *The Roots and Growth of the Common Law.*

been adopted into the usages of the people and grown into law; such adoption being the process by which living law grows.

So the jurists whose writings are authority for international law relied in solving a new question on their own intuition of right, giving as their reason, "*Quia æquum est.*"

So, also, in England, the Chancellors who originated equitable rules overruling law saw, by their intuitive perception, the iniquity of the law to be overruled, and introduced the remedy; and amongst the Judges at Common Law, Hale, Holt, and Mansfield may be taken as examples of men who by the exercise of the same intuitive perception became eminent. They were masters of the learning of their predecessors; their commissions ran then as now, "to do what to justice appertained, according to the laws and customs of England;" and although they maintained in accordance with those laws and customs some of the feudal principles established after the Conquest, which had survived to their time, yet when new relations in social progress raised new questions, and feudality had either expired or was irrelevant, they decided according to their own intuition of justice: and they have their eminence because their intuitions have accorded with those of the strong men in the generations that have succeeded. Mansfield takes rank as a benefactor of mankind; and the recommendation of Junius that he should be impeached for introducing notions of substantial justice to modify some supposed rules of common law which worked iniquity, is evidence of his title to that rank.

CHAP. I. Common Law

§ 6. *The Roots and Growth of the Common Law.*

I have said so much of the common law in general, as well as of those principles thereof which are relevant to trade unions, because the power of the law lies in the respect of the people for it, and I believe that the common law will be regarded as a valuable inheritance by all who understand its principles, and can compare reasoning thereon with reasoning on the mere words of a statute.

There is a description of the sources of the common law by Parke, B., in Mirehouse *v.* Rennell (1 Cl. & Finn. 546), which is superior to any that I can write. Lord Coke, also, has given an account of the sources of the common law in Co. Litt. 11*b*. I pass these descriptions with the remark that they describe rather the places where the stream of the common law may be found flowing, than the place where the source rises or the root begins.

In concluding this chapter, I would refer, for the purpose of removing an unjust estimation

CHAP. I. Common Law.

§ 6. *The Roots and Growth of the Common Law.*

of law, to Hooker's words (*Eccles. Pol.* book i. ch. i.) on *Government*, as equally applicable to law: "He that goeth about to persuade a multitude, that they are not so well governed as they ought to be, shall never want attentive and favourable hearers; because they know the manifold defects whereunto every kind of regiment is subject; but the secret lets and difficulties, which in public proceedings, are innumerable and inevitable, they have not ordinarily the judgment to consider." And for the purpose of a just estimation of our Legislature since the Reform Act of 1832, I refer to Mr. Ludlow, who, in the book by him and Mr. Lloyd Jones on the *Progress of the Working Class from* 1832 *to* 1867, says that the legislation during that time has been "wholesome, stimulant, and beneficent," and justifies these words by specifying numerous statutes of enlightened wisdom and grand beneficent results, both to society in general and to the less rich part of it in particular; wherefrom an ever-rising tide of improvement has been continuously flowing abroad upon the whole body of the people, without a suspicion of partiality for any class.

CHAPTER II.

STATUTE LAW RELATING TO TRADE UNIONS.

*

§ 1. *Statutes prior to 6 Geo. IV. c. 129.*

I. *Statutes prior to 6 George IV. c.* 129.—With respect to the statutes relating to trade unions, the 6 Geo. IV. c. 129, and the supplementary Act 22 Vict. c. 34, are the statutes now in force.

The repealed legislation concerning trade and industry has been blamed for partiality. An examination of the grounds for blame would not now be worth the time, but I would suggest that persons are not justified in imputing it who have not examined the statutes by the light of the times in which they were passed, and are not sure that they could have proposed something more just and expedient if they had been then in Parliament. Much of this legislation was directed against combinations: it was supposed to contain more prohibitions than were required for the protection of person and property, and was all repealed either before

CHAP. II. Statutes.

§ 1. *Statutes prior to 6 Geo. IV. c. 129.*

or by the 5 Geo. IV. c. 95. The framers of this statute seem to have considered that the evils which pressed on the lower stratum of industry before the acts for the reform of Parliament, of the Poor Laws, and of the Corn Laws, would be alleviated by allowing them to combine for the obstruction of the free course of trade, assuming that the employers were richer, and oppressive because richer, and that the working men stood in no need of protection from each other; assuming also that working men could violate the law for truth with impunity, inasmuch as the statute authorised them to combine to induce other working men to break their contracts for service. The evils resulting in one year from this statute were sufficient to produce its repeal, and the substitution of the 6 Geo. IV. c. 129.

§ 2. *The Statute 6 Geo. IV. c. 129.*

II. *The Statute* 6 *George IV. c.* 129.—This statute, like all others, must be construed with reference to the state of the law existing at the time of the enactment, and to the matters recited in the preamble.

The principles of the common law existing at the time have been stated above.

The preamble recites that the provisions of 5 Geo. IV. c. 95 were for the protection of the free employment of capital and labour, and for

§ 2. *The Statute 6 Geo. IV. c. 129.*

the punishment of combinations interfering with such freedom by means of violence, threats, and intimidation, and that the provisions of that statute were not effectual. It then recites that such combinations were dangerous to the tranquillity of the country, and injurious to trade and commerce, and prejudicial to the interest of those concerned in them. It then recites the expediency of making further provision as well for the security and personal freedom of individual workmen in the disposal of their skill and labour, as for the security of the property and persons of the masters and employers.

These recitals show that the Legislature recognized a right to a free course for trade as therein and as herein described, and intended to create further security for the enjoyment of that right without partiality for any class.

Furthermore, it may be noticed that although the 5 Geo. IV. c. 95 contained prohibitions against some combinations, and the attention of the Legislature was upon combinations in passing the 6 Geo. IV. c. 129, yet there is not only no prohibition therein against any kind of combination, but there are, on the contrary, two classes of combinations (those described in ss. 4 and 5) relating to wages, which are thereby rendered exempt from all liability whatever to penal consequences, as well under the common

CHAP. II. Statutes.

§ 2. *The Statute 6 Geo. IV. c. 129.*

as under the statute law: it follows that all combinations and unions which are still unlawful conspiracies are unlawful by the operation of the common law.

The 5 Geo. IV. c. 95 repealed so much of the common law as related to the criminality of the combinations exempted from punishment thereby; the 6 Geo. IV. c. 129 repealed the 5 Geo. IV. c. 95 entirely, and left the common law of conspiracy in force against all combinations in restraint of trade, the combinations exempted from penalty under ss. 4 and 5 alone excepted.

It would be convenient to give here the text of the third, fourth, and fifth sections of the statute 6 Geo. IV. c. 129; but as the important section (the third) is long, and likely to confuse, I print these sections in an Appendix,[1] together with section 44 of 18 & 19 Vict. c. 63, and section 1 of 22 Vict. c. 34, which are hereafter referred to.

(a) The section of 6 Geo. IV. c. 129 containing prohibition.

The operative words of the third section of the Act of 6 Geo. IV. have been arranged with skill in a work on the Law of Combination;[2] and from it I gratefully borrow the subjoined

1 See Appendix B, p. 88.

2 *Strikes and Lock-outs; or, the Law of Combination.* By a Barrister. London, 1867.

§ 2. *The Statute 6 Geo. IV. c. 129.*

analysis, premising that the three classes of the offences created are indicated by Arabic numerals. Each offence consists of an action, together with an effect or purpose: the actions are indicated by letters of the alphabet, and the effects or purposes by Roman numerals.

The offences prohibited by the 6 Geo. IV. c. 129 are all founded upon restraint of trade; and so far this statute declares the common law, while at the same time it adds some summary remedies. In each of the three classes of offences the right to freedom in disposing of labour or capital according to the will of the individual is violated by some coercion, or attempt at coercion, of such will. In the first class the coercion is applied to the working man, in the third it is applied to the employer, and in the second it is applied indifferently to working men or employers in respect of their relation to some union.

The third section enacts as follows:—

"1. If any person,

a. by violence to the person or property,
b. or by molesting,
c. or in any way obstructing another,

i. forces or endeavours to force any journeyman, manufacturer, workman, or other person, hired or employed in any manufacture, trade, or business,

Chap. II. Statutes.

§ 2. *The Statute 6 Geo. IV. c. 129.*

to depart from his hiring, employment, or work,

or to return his work before it is finished,

ii. or prevents or endeavours to prevent any journeyman, manufacturer, workman, or other person, not being hired or employed, from hiring himself to or from accepting work or employment from any person;

every person so offending is liable to three months' imprisonment, with hard labour.

"2. If any person,

a. uses or employs violence to the person or property of another,

b. or uses threats or intimidation,

c. or molests,

d. or in any way obstructs another,

i. for the purpose of forcing or inducing such person to belong to any club or association,

ii. or to contribute to any common fund,

iii. or to pay any fine or penalty,

iv. or on account of his not belonging to any particular club or association,

v. or on account of his not having contributed or having refused to contribute to any common fund, or to pay any fine or penalty,

§ 2. *The Statute 6 Geo. IV. c. 129.*

vi. or on account of his not having complied, or of his refusing to comply with any rules, orders, resolutions, or regulations, made to obtain an advance or to reduce the rate of wages, or to lessen or alter the hours of working, or to decrease or alter the quantity of work, or to regulate the mode of carrying on any manufacture, trade, or business, or the management thereof;

every person so offending is liable to three months' imprisonment, with hard labour.

"3. If any person,

a. by violence to the person or property of another,

b. or by threats or intimidation,

c. or by molesting,

d. or in any way obstructing another,

i. forces, or endeavours to force, any manufacturer, or person carrying on any trade or business,

to make any alteration in his mode of regulating, managing, conducting, or carrying on such manufacture, trade, or business,

or to limit the number of his apprentices, or the number or

Chap. II. Statutes.

§ 2. *The Statute 6 Geo. IV. c. 129.*

description of his journeymen, workmen, or servants;

every person so offending is liable to three months' imprisonment, with hard labour.

"But (s. 4) no persons shall be punished who meet together for the sole purpose of consulting upon and determining the rate of wages or prices, which the persons present at the meeting, or any of them, shall require or demand for their work; or the hours for which they shall work in any manufacture, trade, or business. And (same sec.) no persons shall be punished who enter into any agreement, verbal or written, among themselves, for the purpose of fixing the rate of wages or prices which the parties entering into the agreement, or any of them, shall demand for their work.

"So much for the workmen. The 5th section of the act relates to the masters. By that section the masters are not to be liable to any prosecution or penalty, if they meet together for the sole purpose of consulting upon and determining the rates of wages which those present at the meeting, or any of them, shall pay to their journeymen, workmen, or servants, for their work, or the hours of working, in any manufacture, trade, or business: neither shall they be liable to punishment for entering into any agreement, verbal or written, among themselves, for the purpose of fixing the rate of wages which the parties entering into the agreement, or any of them, shall pay to their journeymen, &c."

§ 2. *The Statute 6 Geo. IV. c. 129.*

In all the classes the elements of the crime, or offence, consist of an act and an intention. In each class, although the offence may be committed either by unionists or by non-unionists, yet the coercion or attempted coercion of the will of the party aggrieved is such as the trade unions, whether of employers or of working men, usually resort to in order to prevent the meeting of supply and demand, of labour and capital, in free competition. Accordingly, the operation of the statute is in practice applied almost entirely to alleged excesses on the part of trade unions.

In the first class, relating to working men, the criminal intention must be to stop work, by preventing either the beginning or the continuance of an employment ; in the third class, relating to employers, the criminal intention must be either to force a change in the management of a business, or to check freedom in the employment of labour ; in the second class, the criminal intention must be on behalf of some union to force either contribution to its funds or compliance with its rules. The terms describing the intention, which is one element of the crime, are clear, and do not appear to have

CHAP. II. Statutes.

§ 2. *The Statute 6 Geo. IV. c. 129.*

led to much dispute, and may be passed without further notice; but the terms describing the act, which is the other element of the crime, have caused doubt.

The acts are described in terms of wide generality, in order that there may be comprehended therein a wide class of actions which from their nature do not admit of precise definition. The essence of the crime lies in the intention to coerce the will of another, indicated by some act comprised under one of the terms "violence," "threats," "intimidation," "molestation," "obstruction;" and the act comprised within either of these terms is sufficient to constitute that element of the crime which lies in action if it was reasonably believed by the party committing it to be such as might coerce the will of the party to be affected thereby.

Violence.

Thus, as to the first term, an act of very slight assault, done for the purpose of assaulting, may be sufficient to prove violence within the meaning of the statute, when such slight assault was intended to be, and was probably, sufficient to coerce the will of a weak and timid person.

Threats.

So also of threats. If any person with the purpose of threatening conveys to the mind of another that he will bring any form of evil upon him, with the intent of forcing him to do one of the acts mentioned in the statute, it seems to me that he has used a threat sufficient to constitute the guilt. The governing object of the statute is to secure the exercise of the free-will of each individual in disposing of his labour or his capital. It matters not what degree of evil may be suggested, if the suggestion is intended to take away free voluntary action as to the matters defined in the statute from the party to whom the suggestion is addressed. Evil may be inflicted in respect of the manifold interests relating to person, property, reputation, or affection. But I say no more on this point, because a material question has been raised—Whether a threat of bringing evil on a party, without otherwise violating any law in so doing, is a threat within the statute? I do not find an express adjudication on this point: as far as I can collect the opinions of the judges from incidental expressions, they appear to preponderate in favour of an answer in the negative.

CHAP. II. Statutes. — § 2. *The Statute 6 Geo. IV. c. 129.*

Intimidation.

What has been said of the class of acts comprised under the term "threat" is true in degree of intimidation. In each class the coercion is intended to be caused by fear: in threats the fear is caused by words; in intimidation, by any deeds or words which might create fear. Whether the acts are sufficient to prove intimidation within the statute ought to depend upon

Chap. II. Statutes.

§ 2. *The Statute 6 Geo. IV. c. 129.*

Molestation.

the degree of timidity on the belief of which the party intending to intimidate acted.

So of acts of molestation. Any act which was intended to cause and did cause annoyance in a substantial degree to the party intended to be molested, if done with one of the prohibited intents, would constitute guilt within the meaning of this term. The measure of the degree of molestation is to be found in the sensibility of the sufferer, not in the act of the actor. By annoyance in a substantial degree, I mean the degree commonly referred to in actions for nuisances. The means of molestation vary infinitely, considering all the channels through which annoyance may be sent to the human mind. Annoyances not sufficient to be an actionable nuisance to the residence, or an actionable damage to the reputation, if they were capable of molesting and were known to be so, and were done for the purpose of molesting with the prohibited intent, would be acts of molestation within the statute, according to my understanding of it.

Obstruction

And so of obstruction. Any act that obstructs the exercise of any right, if done for the purpose of obstructing, and with the prohibited intent, would be sufficient. One frequent mode of committing this offence is by interfering with the right of passage on a high-

Chap. II. Statutes.

§ 2. *The Statute 6 Geo. IV. c. 129.*

way. Every subject has the right to pass and re-pass at all times at his free-will and pleasure, this right being limited by the existence of a similar right in all other subjects; and although the exercise of that similar right may operate as some obstruction to others, still it does not become unlawful thereby if done for the purpose of exercising the right, and if done in the degree reasonable for the exercise of that right. The right and the limitation are constantly exemplified in the uninterrupted passage of any crowd, either of passengers, or of animals, or of carriages, where each uses the passage for himself with attention to the rights of passage for others. But if a person comes on a highway for any purpose other than that of passage, he is a trespasser; and so the use of the highway for the purpose of shooting rabbits thereon was held to be a trespass (see R. *v.* Pratt, 4 Ell. & Bl. 860). So, also, trespass lies for bringing cattle along a highway for the purpose of pasture, and not of passage. According to this doctrine, any use of the highway not for the purpose of lawful passage, but for the purpose of making passengers in any degree unwilling to pass to and from the premises of any party, with the intent of coercing the will of that party, and so of forcing him to do one of the acts specified in the statute, would be a criminal

CHAP. II. Statutes.

§ 2. *The Statute 6 Geo. IV. c. 129.*

obstruction within the statute. Thus if a crowd were assembled in such numbers as to fill the street where the entrance to the premises was, and passed backwards and forwards so as to stop all access, with any other intent than that of using the right of passage, they would be guilty of an offence against the public by a criminal obstruction of the highway, and of an injury to the party to whose premises access was prevented, if he suffered special damage. They would also be guilty of an offence under the statute if they did so with intent to coerce the will of the party having any interest in such premises, and so to force him to one of the acts specified in the statute. These principles, and this interpretation of the statute, were enforced by Bramwell, B. in the cases of R. *v.* Druitt and R. *v.* Partridge (C. C. C. Aug. 21 and 22, 1867; 10 Cox C. C. 592), where the defendants had been concerned in the practice of picketing in the tailors' strike then pending.

And that which is true of a crowd so assembled with the intent of causing an obstruction, and so of coercing the will as above described, is equally true of one person stationed as a watch to give warning, or the like, to persons passing to and from the premises of the party whose will is to be coerced, if he thereby obstructs unlawfully the enjoyment of the right of free

Chap. II. Statutes.

§ 2. *The Statute 6 Geo. IV. c. 129.*

passage for him and others, with intent to coerce his will and force him to one of the specified acts. The amount of actual obstruction is no more material in this offence than the extent of actual removal of a chattel is material in larceny. The smallest wrongful act which is one of the series of acts by which the crime is to be completed externally, coupled with the criminal intention, is the misdemeanour of attempting to commit a crime. In burglary, the breaking may be by the lifting of a latch, and the entrance may be by inserting the tip of a finger. According to this doctrine, the placing of pickets, as they are called, with the usual purpose of interfering with free passage by molesting, or the like, if done with one of the prohibited intents, is the crime of obstruction within the statute. It may also be at the same time the crime of molestation, or of threat, or of intimidation, within the statute; it may also be a wrongful obstruction of the highway at common law, according to the circumstances; and may be actionable and indictable.

I will further suggest that the words prohibiting "molestation" and "obstruction," as well as violence, intimidation, and threats, are to be taken in their common acceptation, not limited by the words that precede. These

CHAP. II. Statutes.

§ 2. *The Statute 6 Geo. IV. c. 129.*

two terms are additional to those in 5 Geo. IV. c. 95, and the Legislature must be taken to have added them with the intention that they should be so construed as to receive effect according to their ordinary acceptation.

The description of the offences prohibited by the third section of 6 Geo. IV. c. 129 creates a difficulty in enforcing the statute, inasmuch as they are made to consist of an intentional act of grievance, with an ulterior intention to cause an act to be done by the party wronged. Thus, if an offence by molestation is taken as an example, there must be an act of molestation against the employer with intention to molest him—as by taking his men away—with an ulterior intention to force him to alter his mode of carrying on business—as by paying wages according to a book. Intention as an element of crime is more difficult of proof than acts of crime, and becomes more so in proportion as it is less closely connected with the act which is the other element of crime. The complications of statement required in indicting for a crime consisting of two intentions is seen in the twenty counts of the indictment for conspiracy to commit offences against this statute in R. *v.* Rowlands (5 Cox C. C. 436).

There is a further difficulty in applying the statute by reason that the description of the

§ 2. *The Statute 6 Geo. IV. c. 129.*

classes of actions by the supposed wrong-doer, which are to constitute that element of the offence which lies in act, as contradistinguished from intention, consists more of the effect of that action upon another, than of the deed done by the wrong-doer himself. In respect of the first three classes—violence, threats, and intimidation—this remark is true to some extent, though practically acts of violence, threatening, or intimidation, can be recognised without difficulty. As to the remaining two classes—viz., molestation and obstruction—the description by which the guiltiness of the action imputed as the act of the offence can be tested, refers solely to the effect of the action either upon the feelings or upon the rights of the opposite party. The description, therefore, is wide enough to include every word or deed spoken or done for the purpose of molesting or obstructing, and producing the purposed effect, with one of the prohibited ulterior intents specified in the statute. In respect of acts causing obstruction, the difficulty is less than in the case of molestation. Nevertheless, the prohibition against molestation has very important effects towards securing freedom from constraint.

(b) The Sections of 6 Geo IV. c. 129 for permission.

Sections 4 and 5,[1] the substance of which has been already given, are sections of permission,

[1] See the text of these sections in Appendix B, p. 88.

CHAP. II. Statutes.

§ 2. *The Statute 6 Geo. IV. c.* 129.

giving impunity to some combinations theretofore illegal.

The principles of the common law have been above considered.

The third section of the statute 6 Geo. IV. c. 129 enumerates certain violations of the right to free trade which are unlawful at common law as well as by this statute; and in respect of these violations of free trade it enacts that there should be a summary remedy, as before explained; then ss. 4 and 5 grant impunities in respect of the combinations therein mentioned, which are assumed to be illegal for restraint of trade, but which are exempted thereby from punishment.

The fourth section exempts from any penal consequences as well meetings to consult on the wages which the persons present at the meeting shall accept, as any agreement respecting the wages which the persons entering into such agreement shall receive. Under this section unions can with impunity combine with respect to the wages and hours of the parties either present at the meeting or entering into the agreement. As the exemption is limited to parties present at a meeting, or entering into the agreement personally, it may be held that this power of combining for wages was intended to be confined to unions for a limited district, where the rate of wages, and the cost of

Chap. II. Statutes.

§ 2. *The Statute 6 Geo. IV. c. 129.*

living, and other circumstances affecting a rate of wages, might be uniform, and was not intended to apply to extensive unions or amalgamations of unions. But it is a question of construction on which I find no adjudication.[1] It gives to the workmen's unions within the exemption the power to combine for regulating the rate of the members' wages, but excludes them from interference in respect of the mode of carrying on business, or of the number of apprentices or journeymen, or of piecework, and other trade matters; and by s. 5 the same provisions, *mutatis mutandis*, are applied to masters.

It should be borne in mind that the impunity is limited to combinations for the purpose of directly raising or lowering wages, as described in the section, and does not extend to combinations immediately for crimes and mediately through those crimes for a rise of wages. Combinations to exclude apprentices, piecework, and overtime are indirectly to increase wages, but the words of exemption do not in my opinion extend to such combinations.

As the unions, although coming within the exemption from punishment, remain unlawful if they operate in unlawful restraint of trade,

[1] Since this was written the Amalgamated Society of Carpenters has been held to be legal, no objection being taken on the ground of amalgamation. (Farrer *v.* Close, Q. B., Jan. 18, 1868.)

CHAP. II. Statutes.

§ 2. *The Statute 6 Geo. IV. c. 129.*

one consequence of illegality is that any member of the union is free to leave the union at any moment, and that he cannot make himself liable by his agreement to fines or other bad consequences for leaving. The members of such unions act in combination as long as they choose, and leave the combination whenever they choose. And although a combination merely for the purpose of raising wages is permitted by the statute, and a simultaneous stop from work of several men really intended for that purpose is permitted, yet a simultaneous stop for the immediate purpose of inflicting a loss upon an employer, and so of coercing his will, with an ulterior view of raising wages, does not seem to me to be permitted thereby; as for instance, if the stop was planned for the purpose of drowning a mine, or extinguishing the fire of a smelting furnace, or stopping all traffic on a railway, and so of causing loss, such a stop might amount to molestation and obstruction under the statute, and might be a conspiracy at common law, and not protected by sections 4 and 5.

If this important statute had made lawful the combinations which it exempted from punishment, the improvement would have been very great, and the law would thereby have been made to be as it was supposed to be by

Erle, J. in Hilton *v.* Eckersley, above mentioned.

CHAP. II Statutes.

§ 3. *The Statute 22 Vict. c. 34.*

III. *The Statute 22 Victoria, c.* 34.—I am not aware that this statute has received any judicial construction, and will only venture to offer one or two observations.[1]

It was passed, as appears from the preamble, both to declare and to further the intention of 6 George IV. c. 129, s. 4, in consequence of some decision supposed to require correction, probably a ruling of some point in R. *v.* Rowlands and R. *v.* Duffield, of which cases some account is given in the Appendix.[2] Its operation is limited to give impunity to other persons besides workmen (1) for meeting with workmen and agreeing upon a rate of wages to be claimed by them, and (2) for endeavouring peaceably and without intimidation to persuade others—that is, other workmen—to cease or abstain from work in order to obtain the rate of wages so agreed on or to be agreed on. Therefore, persons other than workmen cannot claim impunity under this statute, unless they act with workmen meeting in accordance with the provisions of 6 Geo. IV. c. 129, s. 4; nor as to persuading to cease from work, unless there be an agreement and

[1] See the section of the statute in Appendix B, p. 91.
[2] See Appendix A, p. 81.

Chap. II. Statutes.

an unsettled claim thereon in respect of wages, also in accordance with the statute of 6 Geo. IV.

§ 3. *The Statute 22 Vict. c. 34.*

Moreover, the act gives impunity for the actions above mentioned, so far as the statute 6 Geo. IV. c. 129, s. 3, and the law against conspiracy, are concerned. The parties coming within the provisions of this act still remain liable to action for any civil injuries for violating rights to the free course for labour, as well as liable to the remedies for criminal wrongs other than those specified in the statute, notwithstanding its provisions.

§ 4. *The Statute 18 & 19 Vict. c. 63, s. 44.*

IV. *The Statute 18 & 19 Victoria, c. 63, s. 44 (the Friendly Societies Act).*—There remains the question, whether the societies exempted from liabilities to punishment by 6 Geo. IV. c. 129, ss. 4 and 5, are entitled to the benefits respecting security for property and settlement of disputes which were granted to societies established "for any purpose which is not illegal" under the Friendly Societies Act.[1]

The operation of 6 Geo. IV. c. 129, ss. 4 and 5, seems to be this:—The unions exempted from liability to any penal consequences thereby have power to combine for the objects therein mentioned, and to collect funds by voluntary contributions, with impunity. But in respect of

[1] See the section of the Statute in Appendix B, p. 90.

the unions which obtain exemption from punishment by reason of those sections, it follows that they operate in restraint of trade, and are illegal, and that illegality is not affected by the exemption from penal consequences.

§ 4. *The Statute 18 & 19 Vict. c. 63, s. 44.*

Hornby v. Close.

In Hornby *v.* Close (10 Cox C. C. 393), it was held, first, that the trade union there mentioned was not within the Act (18 & 19 Vict. c. 63, s. 44), because it was not *ejusdem generis* with a friendly society (but that point is no longer material); and secondly, that a society or union was established for an illegal purpose where the rules operated in illegal restraint of trade, and that, if it was established for an illegal purpose, it could not take the benefit granted by the Act to societies established for any purpose not illegal. In that case rules against piecework were held to be in illegal restraint of trade.

This construction of the 44th section appears to have caused disappointment, but perhaps that feeling would be abated if the words of the statute were considered together with the rules of law operating therewith, without assuming that the intention was to give to trade unions the benefit of the summary jurisdiction given for friendly societies.

It is essential for the exercise of summary jurisdiction by an inferior tribunal that the

CHAP. II. Statutes

§ 4. *The Statute 18 & 19 Vict. c. 63, s. 44.*

event, on the happening of which the jurisdiction is to attach, should be defined. This has been clearly done in respect of friendly societies, but in respect of trade unions the operative words are, that a society "established for any purpose which is not illegal" may claim aid from the summary jurisdiction. Then arises the question—What is a "society" within the meaning of this section? The term is wide enough to include trade unions, but it also includes every concert of two or more to act together, and therefore includes more than can have been intended. If the excess is to be limited to societies *ejusdem generis* with friendly societies, the rule is grievously vague.

But assuming that a trade union may be a society within the Act, if it is not for an illegal purpose, what are the "purposes" of a society? As a society it has no mind, and the beginning of its action must be by resolution of the whole or the governing part of the members; and if the purposes are only those which are declared by resolution, the provision against illegal purposes is almost nullified, as they might not be declared. But whether the purposes are those expressed in resolutions, or secretly entertained, how is the magistrate to ascertain their existence? And yet he must do so at his peril before he exercises the jurisdiction, unless it should be held that the purposes are presumed to be legal till that presumption be rebutted by evidence. In the case of Hornby *v.* Close, these difficulties as to ascertaining the purposes of the society were removed, because the rules were produced, and were held to operate in restraint of trade, inasmuch as they prohibited piecework under pain of fine and expulsion.

CHAP. II Statutes.

§ 4. *The Statute 18 & 19 Vict. c.* 63. *s.* 44.

The effect of this case has been misunderstood if it is supposed to decide that the members of trade unions have not all the ordinary remedies for violations of rights of property which the members of the community in general possess. They have difficulties from the shifting of members, and from joint ownership, as explained above ; but they may proceed by action or indictment where other subjects would have a right to do so, and in those proceedings the legality or illegality of their purposes is immaterial. They might have also the benefits of incorporation, and therewith all the powers of the law to enforce their rules, and protect their rights, if they would take the law to be as it is laid down by the competent tribunals, and alter their rules conformably thereto.

Farrer v. Close.

Since the above was written, it has been decided in Farrer *v.* Close (Q.B. January 18, 1868),

CHAP. II. Statutes.

§ 4. *The Statute 18 & 19 Vict. c. 63. s. 44.*

that the Amalgamated Society of Carpenters was entitled to the benefit of the 44th section of the Friendly Societies' Act, against an officer who had misappropriated the money of the society. The rules authorized the application of the funds to various trade purposes, and among others to the support of members when out of work; and although it was objected that the funds might thus be applied to maintain strikes, it was said that a strike was not necessarily illegal; and the case was distinguished from Hornby *v.* Close, because there was no rule operating directly in restraint of trade, such as the rule prohibiting piecework in the latter case. The inferences from the judgment in Farrer *v.* Close seem important for the interests of trade unions, as regards both the recognition of the legality of some strikes, and the indication of the boundary between legal and illegal purposes within the meaning of this section.

APPENDIX A.

SOME ACCOUNT OF THE TRIALS OF R. *v.* ROWLANDS AND OTHERS, AND R. *v.* DUFFIELD AND OTHERS (5 COX C. C. 436 AND 404).

*

ON the trial of these cases the judge said certain things to the jury which have since been cited as if he laid down propositions of law absolutely. But in all cases it is essential for the correct understanding of the words of a judge to bear in mind the facts to which they relate.

APPENDIX A

R. *v.* Rowlands and R. *v.* Duffield.

The account of the trial may be of use in showing the meaning of the ruling, and in exemplifying the importance of security under the law for the disposing of labour as well as capital.

I describe the facts according to the effect of the evidence on my mind. In 1849, in Wolverhampton, there were six firms of tin-plate workers and japanners, who made and japanned tin-plate articles. Without understanding the manufacture, I assume for the purpose of this case that some of these articles could be made by hand with three processes, viz. punching holes, cutting out pieces, and joining the pieces; and that some of these firms possessed machinery for some of these processes, Messrs. Perry making more use of machinery than their rivals. The workmen in Wolverhampton were usually paid by the article, so much for a cullender or a pepper-box. Some of the Wolverhampton unions had proposed a book of prices,

APPENDIX A.

R. v. Rowlands and R. v. Duffield.

which were to be uniform for each article; but as the proper wages for workmen who did all processes by hand, if paid on this principle, would be too much for workmen who did some processes only by hand and some by machinery, and as the wages claimed were not supposed to be properly adjusted according to the use of machinery, the two firms of the Messrs. Perry did not consent to pay according to the proposed book of prices; but they paid such prices that their workmen received for their time more than workmen for other firms who were paid according to the book. The Messrs. Perry prospered, and their workmen were well off and contented; but as they undersold the rival manufacturers, and as they superseded hand-labour by machinery, there were two sources of hostility towards them.

In November 1849, Messrs. Perry and Son, one of the firms, saw reason to be dissatisfied with a workman named Preston, and discharged him.

There was a National Association of United Trades in London, of which the defendant Peel was secretary, the defendant Green a delegate, and the defendant Winters a member. The other defendants were members of provincial unions; but not one of them was employed by Messrs. Perry, or had any monied interest at stake in the strike, as far as I could perceive. The reserve fund of the National Association was stated to be more than 20,000*l.*, and Preston, it was said, had contributed and procured contributions thereto. Preston seems to have applied to this association in respect of his discharge by his employers.

The following is the account by Mr. George Henry Perry of the setting in of the strike:—

Appendix A.

R. v. Rowlands and R. v. Duffield.

"I am a manufacturer at Wolverhampton, carrying on business under the firm of Perry and Son. I have carried it on for twenty years, and my father did before me. In the spring of 1850 I had 120 men, half for tin work, half for japan. The japan workers depend on the tin workers. During the first three months of 1850 we were in good work with large orders. The workmen's wages would range from 25*s.* to 50*s.*, but some earned 60*s.* In November 1849 I discharged Thomas Preston. I was not aware of any differences between me and my workmen in the spring of 1850. We had been comfortable for many years before we received a certain letter.

"In the second week of December, 1849, Green called about Preston. He stated he was a member of the National Association of United Trades, of which Thomas Duncombe, M.P. was president, that they had considerable funds (20,000*l.* I believe) at the delegates' command, and that nearly the entire working population was co-operating with them. I said, 'Mr. Green, what is your business with me?' He replied, 'You've discharged Thomas Preston; I've called to know the reason.' I said we did not require Preston's services, that was our reason for discharging him. He asked if it was not because he belonged to the club that we discharged him. (The club is the Tin-plate Workers' Society.) I said the reason we discharged him was because we did not want his services. He again asked if it was not because he belonged to the club; if it was, *they should take all the men out; they should stop the supplies, so that not a man should call.* He then left me with the assurance from me that we discharged Preston because we did not want

Appendix A.

R. v. Rowlands and R. v. Duffield.

his services. The question I put was this, that he had better mind his own business, and not come meddling and interfering with ours. He did not mention any name then. Nothing else passed that I recollect.

"I received a letter about the 3d of April, which was dated 2d April, 1850, headed 'Selling-book of prices,' and signed

"'FREDK. GREEN, } *Mediators, not in an*
"'THOS. WINTERS, } *offensive spirit.*'

[The letter was produced and read.]

"After I had received this letter Green called about the 12th April. He said he was a delegate from the National Association, and he and Mr. Peel had come down to settle the difference between us and our workmen. I told him that I was not aware there was any difference between us and our men, and that if our men had anything to complain of, and would come to me, we could settle it without his interference; and begged that he would not come meddling with our business. He then said he wished us to adopt a book of prices which the men had written out, and of which a copy had been sent us. I said I had not had an opportunity of looking at the list, but I would do so in a few days of leisure. Nothing else occurred.

"He called again in a week or fortnight. He again urged me to adopt this book of prices, and said if we did not they should take all the men out. As we had very large orders for America unexecuted, I did not tell him pointedly we would not pay the book, but that we would consider of it, so as to get time and to get some more men hired. I did not wish to have the men taken out. Nothing else occurred."

The sequel of the evidence describes the course of

APPENDIX A

R. v. Rowlands and R. v. Duffield.

the strike. If I rightly appreciate it, it shows the power of evil in remorseless activity, destroying those relations between employers and employed on which comfort and peace depend, bringing guilt and misery on the workmen and ruin on their employers. The Messrs. Perry maintained their right for freedom for the course of labour with energy. Hoping for support according to law, they tried all the resources for labour in England. They tried to go on with apprentices and boys, and twice imported a band of artisans from France. But in vain; their factories were deserted, and their trade stopped.

The workmen were induced, some to break their contracts, others to leave their employ without notice. Pickets at every approach were busy with all that came and went; money was paid largely to get workmen away—600*l.* for the removal of the Frenchmen alone. Some of the men were supplied with liquor and induced to go to the railway station, and to enter a carriage without knowing the purpose. They were conveyed to different places, where a scanty supply of money was sent for a few weeks, and then many were left to themselves; their discomfort may be imagined from the case of two workmen who, being left penniless, walked home fifty-two miles without a farthing to support them, and were so blamed for returning that the wife of one of them had to stop the coarse abuse upon her husband by threatening to use a brush handle to drive them out of the house.

But the guilt towards the apprentices was worse; not only were they taught to disregard their contracts and to abscond, but one of the defendants was stated to have made a suggestion "that apprentices could do

Appendix A.

R. v. Rowlands and R. v. Duffield.

them great service if they would; he remembered when he was connected with leather what game the apprentices played in cutting up and destroying leather; and the foreman of Messrs. Perry deposed that before the apprentices went away the tools were injured, the tin was cut to waste, and the patterns were missing. After the close of the strike a party of apprentices were said to have been found huddled in a garret in London.

This misery was inflicted by parties, many of whom seemed ill qualified to appreciate the importance of the matter in dispute. Judging from outward appearances, the London defendants were men of high respectability, with intellect and experience qualifying them to discern at a glance the essence of any transaction they were engaged in, and to guide the course of it; the provincial defendants seemed to be little more than instruments in their hands. It was not clear that there was any monied interest at stake; some of the witnesses said that wages according to the book would be lower than the current rate without the book. It is not probable that the president of the association understood or cared for useful industry, or that their secretary or delegate understood about the book of prices, if the description of the question respecting the book was correctly given by Mr. Perry. But it may be that the dragging of two well-established firms of manufacturers down from a station of wealth and influence through various stages to ruin would be an impressive warning not to trust to the law for help against a trade union; it may be that there was a probability of increased subscriptions if a master was sacrificed for discharging a servant; it may also be that the defendants believed they were promoting the interest of working men. Motives are never matter of certain knowledge. According as the motives should be found honest or corrupt so would the liability be, if the principles here stated are correct.

APPENDIX A.

R. *v.* Rowlands and R. *v.* Duffield.

It was at the close of the trial that the judge used some of the words which have been brought into question, first informing the jury, in effect, that they were not trying workmen for combining to obtain a rise of their own wages, and then stating that they were trying the defendants for other and different offences, as set forth in the indictment; and, among other things, ruling that there was evidence to go to the jury against Winters and Rowlands, although the only overt acts of conspiracy in evidence against them were acts of persuading men while the strike was going on to leave Messrs. Perry's employ, without using threats or intimidation.

The case of R. *v.* Rowlands is in substance the same as R. *v.* Duffield; in the one the defendants struck against Messrs. Perry and Son, in the other they struck against the firm of Mr. Edward Perry. The question of the book was the ground of the strike against both firms, and both firms rejected the book for the reason above explained.

The facts of this case, taken with the reasoning of the foregoing Memorandum, raise two questions: first, Did every member of the executive committee in London, who authorised Messrs. Green and Peel to take part in the strike, incur the same criminal guilt as Messrs. Green and Peel? and secondly, Was every such member of that committee liable in an action by every person who suffered damage from that strike, and was every such person entitled to recover therein the amount of such damage?

APPENDIX B.

SECTIONS 3, 4, 5, OF THE ACT 6 GEO. IV. C. 129.

6 Geo. IV. c. 129, ss. 3, 4, 5.

Penalty on Persons compelling Journeymen to leave their Employment, or to return Work unfinished;

III. And be it further enacted, That from and after the passing of this Act, if any Person shall by Violence to the Person or Property, or by Threats or Intimidation, or by molesting or in any way obstructing another, force or endeavour to force any Journeyman, Manufacturer, Workman, or other Person hired or employed in any Manufacture, Trade, or Business, to depart from his Hiring, Employment, or Work, or to return his Work before the same shall be finished, or prevent or endeavour to prevent any Journeyman, Manufacturer, Workman, or other Person not being hired or employed from hiring himself to, or from accepting Work or Employment from any Person or Persons; or if any Person shall use or employ Violence to the Person or Property of another, or Threats or Intimidation, or shall molest or in any way obstruct another for the Purpose of forcing or inducing such Person to belong to any Club or Association, or to contribute to any common Fund, or to pay any Fine or Penalty, or on account of his not belonging to any particular Club or Association, or not having contributed or having refused to contribute to any common Fund, or to pay any Fine or Penalty, or on account of his not having complied or of his refusing to comply with any

or preventing their Hiring themselves;

or compelling them to belong to Clubs, &c.;

or to pay any Fines, for not having

Rules, Orders, Resolutions, or Regulations made to obtain an Advance or to reduce the Rate of Wages, or to lessen or alter the Hours of Working, or to decrease or alter the Quantity of Work, or to regulate the Mode of carrying on any Manufacture, Trade, or Business, or the Management thereof; or if any Person shall by Violence to the Person or Property of another, or by Threats or Intimidation, or by molesting or in any way obstructing another, force or endeavour to force any Manufacturer or Person carrying on any Trade or Business, to make any Alteration in his Mode of regulating, managing, conducting, or carrying on such Manufacture, Trade, or Business, or to limit the Number of his Apprentices, or the Number or Description of his Journeymen, Workmen, or Servants; every Person so offending, or aiding, abetting, or assisting therein, being convicted thereof in Manner herein after mentioned, shall be imprisoned only, or shall and may be imprisoned and kept to Hard Labour, for any Time not exceeding Three Calendar Months.

APPENDIX B.

6 Geo. IV. c. 129, ss. 3, 4, 5.

complied with Orders as to Wages;

or compelling any Manufacturer, &c. to alter his mode of carrying on Business;

Imprisonment, or Imprisonment with Hard Labour for Three Months.

IV. Provided always, and be it enacted, That this Act shall not extend to subject any Persons to Punishment who shall meet together for the sole Purpose of consulting upon and determining the Rate of Wages or Prices, which the Persons present at such Meeting or any of them, shall require or demand for his or their Work, or the Hours or Time for which he or they shall work in any Manufacture, Trade, or Business, or who shall enter into any Agreement, verbal or written, among themselves, for the Purpose of fixing the Rate of Wages of Prices which the Parties entering into such Agreement, or any of them, shall re-

Not to affect Meetings for settling Rates of Wages to be received, or Hours of Work to be employed by the Persons meeting.

APPENDIX B.

6 Geo. IV. c. 129, ss. 3, 4, 5.

quire or demand for his or their work, or the Hours of Time for which he or they will work, in any Manufacture, Trade, or Business; and that Persons so meeting for the Purposes aforesaid, or entering into any such Agreement as aforesaid, shall not be liable to any Prosecution or Penalty for so doing; any Law or Statute to the contrary notwithstanding.

Not to affect Meetings for Rates of Wages, &c. to be paid by Masters to Journeymen, &c.

V. Provided also, and be it further enacted, That this Act shall not extend to subject any Persons to Punishment who shall meet together for the sole Purpose of consulting upon and determining the Rate of Wages or Prices which the Persons present at such Meeting, or any of them, shall pay to his or their Journeyman, Workmen, or Servants, for their Work, or the Hours or Time of working in any Manufacture, Trade, or Business, or who shall enter into any Agreement, verbal or written, among themselves, for the Purpose of fixing the Rate of Wages or Prices, which the Parties entering into such Agreement, or any of them, shall pay to his or their Journeymen, Workmen, or Servants, for their Work, or the Hours or Time of working in any Manufacture, Trade, or Business; and that Persons so meeting for the Purposes aforesaid, or entering into any such Agreement as aforesaid, shall not be liable to any Prosecution or Penalty for so doing, any Law or Statute to the contrary notwithstanding.

SECTION 44 OF THE ACT 18 & 19 VICT. C. 63.

18 & 19 Vict. c. 63, s. 44.

In the Case of Societies

XLIV. In the case of any Friendly Society established for any of the Purposes mentioned in Section IX. of this Act, or for any Purpose which is not illegal, having written or printed Rules, whose Rules have not been certified by the Registrar, provided a Copy of such Rules shall have been deposited with the Registrar, every Dispute between any Member or Members of such Society, and the Trustees, Treasurer, or other Officer, or the Committee of such Society, shall be decided in manner herein-before provided with respect to Disputes, and the Decision thereof, in the Case of Societies to be established under this Act, and the Sections in this Act provided for such Decision and also the Section in this Act which enacts a Punishment in case of Fraud or Imposition by an Officer, Member, or Person, shall be applicable to such uncertified Societies: Provided always, that nothing herein contained shall be construed to confer on any such Society whose Rules shall not have been certified by the Registrar, or any of the Members or Officers of such Society, any of the Powers, Exemptions, or Facilities of this Act, save and except as in and by this Section is expressly provided.

APPENDIX B.

18 & 19 Vict. c. 63, s. 44.

whose Rules are not certified, Disputes between the Society and its own Members to be settled as in Cases of certified Societies.

SECTION 1 OF THE ACT 22 VICT. C. 34.

I. That no Workman or other Person, whether actually in Employment or not, shall, by reason merely of his entering into an Agreement with any Workman or Workmen, or other Person or Persons, for the purpose of fixing or endeavouring to fix the Rate of Wages or Remuneration at which they or any of them shall work, or by reason merely of his endeavouring peaceably, and in a reasonable Manner, and without Threat or Intimidation, direct or indirect, to persuade

22 Vict. c. 34, s. 1.

Agreements in certain Cases not to be deemed "Molestation" or "Obstruction."

APPENDIX B.

22 Vict. c. 34, s. 1.

within the Meaning of the recited Act.

others to cease or abstain from Work in order to obtain the Rate of Wages or the altered Hours of Labour so fixed or agreed upon or to be agreed upon, shall be deemed or taken to be guilty of "Molestation" or "Obstruction," within the Meaning of the said Act, and shall not therefore be subject or liable to any Prosecution or Indictment for Conspiracy: Provided always, that nothing herein contained shall authorize any Workman to break or depart from any Contract or authorize any Attempt to induce any Workman to break or depart from any Contract.

THE END.

LONDON: R. CLAY, SONS, AND TAYLOR, PRINTERS.

www.ingramcontent.com/pod-product-compliance
Lightning Source LLC
Chambersburg PA
CBHW020158170426
43199CB00010B/1097
9783744727525